THE WIFE OF THE LEFT HAND

THE WIFE OF THE LEFT HAND

NANCY KUHL

Published in the United Kingdom in 2007 by Shearsman Books Ltd
58 Velwell Road
Exeter EX4 4LD
www.shearsman.com

ISBN-13   978-1-905700-06-6

ISBN-10   1-905700-06-7

Copyright © Nancy Kuhl, 2007.

The right of Nancy Kuhl to be identified as the author of this work has been asserted by her in accordance with the Copyrights, Designs and Patents Act of 1988. All rights reserved. No part of this publication may be reproduced, stored in a retrieval system, transmitted in any form or by any means, electronic, mechanical, photocopying, recording or otherwise, without the prior permission of the publisher.

Photo of the author on page 69 by David D. Driscoll

DESIGN Megan Mangum, Words That Work

The publisher gratefully acknowledges financial
assistance from Arts Council England.

for Richard

And I look at my distant words.
They are more yours than mine.
—Pablo Neruda

TABLE OF CONTENTS

ALMANAC	1
ON SUMMER STREET	2
THE WIFE OF THE LEFT HAND	3
WEDDING PARTY	5
A BIOGRAPHY OF SALOME	6
THE AFFAIR OF THE FIRE EATERS	10
PANELS: THE DINNER PARTY	11
PRAYER FOR THE INSOMNIAC	16
THE SWAY OF ORDINARY LIGHT	17

HIGH STREET	21
PECCADILLOES	22
SHOULD SALOME APOLOGIZE	23
HOLIDAY	24
A BIOGRAPHY OF AMELIA EARHART	25
ADVICE FOR THE BRIDE	28
THE ORDINARY HUSBAND	30
UPON CROSSING THE THRESHOLD, THE BRIDE	32

PYRAMID	35
SHE ASKS	37

HOUSE GEOMETRY 38
SALOME'S ANSWER 39
APOLOGY FOR NEW WIVES 40
SALOME AND JOHN THE BAPTIST 41
OFF AT THE HINGES 44
KEYS 45

CURSING THE EQUATOR 48
THE CATHERINE WHEEL 51
FRESH PAINT IN EVERY ROOM 53
WINDOWS 55
SALOME MEANS *PEACE BE WITH YOU* 56
OPEN HOUSE 57
EVERYWHERE AT ONCE 59
THE WIFE OF THE LEFT HAND 62
GHOST TOWN 63

ACKNOWLEDGMENTS

ALMANAC

Midnight tides answer
the new (new coppery
coin new smudge of not
night) the new
October moon.
There is a window. There is
a window and it knocks
in its frame. Everywhere
women press the heels
of hands to eyes. Swaying
and unsteady. The bottle
green depth of the Atlantic
has been calculated
within inches. There are
watermarks six inches above
the baseboards in the parlor.
No wind-burned summer
girls pace thirsty riverbeds
for water glass, colorless.
In August a meteor
shower was promised but
didn't deliver. Bluish clouds
gather in an unfamiliar
arrangement, triangulation
of sky stars sky: blueprint
of who knows what.
Read a sundial; pattern
everything after today's
perfectly horizontal light.
Mercury is visible
in the earliest morning
hours if you know
what you're looking for.

ON SUMMER STREET

Light is a way of organizing
a picture, subjects newly
ordered. At a table before

a window we watch him walk
away, our mud-soaked brother half-
drowned; there was anticipation,

the expectation of a faint pleasure
in the seams of his work shirt; he
lays his subtle indictment at our feet.

We wait. Coffee goes cold. Nearby
a short-skirted pickpocket lifts
billfold, keys on a silver chain.

Sister of our discontent.
Wait. We wait. For what, no one
can be sure. An absence filled

with webs. Time will tell
it has told me all it promised.
The focus of glass, the frame.

This is the narrative of a house
(heartless I am not asleep)
the narrative of a house

with its unswerving spine exposed.

THE WIFE OF THE LEFT HAND

    The backlit town-
    hall clock mistaken
    for a low-hung moon keeps

    the town fast.
    She the consort
    the comely the small getting

    smaller. It is unnatural
    this want for the red
    mark of the second hand.

    Lopsided impressions
    otherwise empty
    air, fish and

    secrets. Hurry and gone
    and you know
    full well cannot

    hold up, cannot bear her
    weight; this is
    the year of without.

    She speaks bluntly
    does not embellish
    nor beautify.

    Those morning girls
    play poolside
    bridge—smooth legs, tennis

skirts and tall glasses; they
sing her to the end
of the line.

Luxury of what
sweet put hands to, can mend.
Oh, little daughter

of the radio
wait and wait
for that suggestive

slip of voice.
Her unhappiness is a blur, a thumb-
smear on a window and

she is becoming
indulgent, sweaty,
a little wicked.

In her house it is
midnight all day.

WEDDING PARTY

    Such a letter of human history, a   song and
    the whole town   singing.

    The bride   is luxury
        and utility she is

    the synonym   of sex.
    She aspires to want   nothing

    not a window or tower   not paintbrushes
    not a slip bolt-   lock. She is newly

    extravagant: *I had red hair and*   *what*
    was I going to do   *with that?* Newly

    sacred.   To marry is twin and
    tangle.   A clear plastic bubble cups

    each pill   hormones suspend
    further mystery.

    In this   city it rains even
    in the hallways

    of fine hotels.   She thought
    she'd move toward

    the skyline
            some inevitable next.

A BIOGRAPHY OF SALOME

1. Salome in Summer

first touch (fingers to
wrist). the humidity
misuses everything, curls
bark away from
tree trunks. first gift (so
memorably red, the
blossom, even as it
wilted and undid
itself). when wind
shifts among
waist-high weeds
and dry shadow, she
knows the seasons
will change. first kiss
(swollen, the bee-
sting on her shoulder
unbearable—the heat
absurd). in haste she
bathes with one hand. the
water will not make her
different but her
skin won't ever
feel like this again.

2. Salome Stares at the Sun

　　The blue inevitable, the circling
　　black rim of not light is

　　the space between what was
　　and what next is (did she

　　know it would be like
　　this?), the shivering

　　moment before sleep when
　　her body vanishes. It is easy

　　to look too long. Eyes
　　slip out of focus, things

　　blur from shape to
　　color. Before the world burns

　　white, she sees the familiar curves
　　of lip, hip, shoulder,

　　the form she loved. The fine
　　hideous body, brown as the drying grass,

　　strikes her as unforgettable
　　in the second before she slides

　　behind the eyelid's
　　veil.

3. One Day is Just like Another

Because when my
mother strokes my hair, when
she pulls her fingers through,
wraps it in a snaking braid, ties it
back, I am the most beautiful
woman in this or any city. From
this window, unfaithful
limbs block my view.
One sees only steps to
the courtyard door, dim
shadow of a man. Never the man.
Because women leave any room I enter.
Because once I nearly drowned and
this doesn't happen to everyone.
Found myself choking and transparent
on the riverbank. Because, after
that, I became reckless. I still taste
sand and clear blue panic. Anyone
can see my arms are strong
as a man's, powerful as
a swan's striking neck. Because
their eyes move over me as casually
as hands travel a glossy banister.
I daily crave a sugary thing
dissolving on my tongue, the
sweet impression. My lover's name

a chant I can't keep myself
from saying. Because we are
talking about midnight.
Saying again. Because the air
in my curtained rooms flashes
clean as eucalyptus. One day.
One day is just like another.
Because I hear them say *she is only*....
I lean from the window each night
to see which moon will rise.

THE AFFAIR OF THE FIRE EATERS

So much better the brittle ash,
better than tearing. So much
seashell gone silent, spiral, translucent

white burn. The chemical smell of it.
A struck match to a photograph—
bubbles, blackens. Run the film

backwards: the fire goes out
when he holds the match to the baton.
What we do we do with the body.

Home movies emptied onto a sheet
hung in the basement. Wife of soot, wife
of burnt hair and the man gone electric.

Everything is soaked in the slippery
smell of gasoline. The woman he loves
holds a drink like you'd hold a pistol.

A joke's a joke so tell it.
The fire eater is reckless, head back
eyes wide open, wide open spilling

red reflection. They can't help but
think of his salt-cooled mouth.
If it's a sideshow, bring them all.

PANELS: THE DINNER PARTY

1. *Still Life with Spilled Red*

   Silver, precisely set, catches gold
   firelight; crystal cuts shadow. This
   table holds everything that keeps her
   rooted here: open-mouthed irises, blinking
   sugar bowl, finger-thin flutes. This room,
   she knows, rests atop a gash in the earth's
   surface where hot mud bubbles nightly from below.

   Wine scrolls across
   the table like calligraphy:
   What more could they want?

2. Portrait of the Hostess

She imagines her husband's
lips closing on the babysitter's
pushy nipple, cool as a dime and
round. She imagines his hand,
without grace or tenderness, under
the girl's tired dress. She does not
know whether or not the girl
wants this, his body pressing
into her own. Meanwhile, the hostess
serves her poultry-colored guests:
speckled guinea hen, peacock,
white pigeon with ugly orange feet.
The babysitter hangs like a mandorla
over her head. The hostess offers
blood oranges with dark vinegar, sliced
pears in deep red raspberry sauce.

3. *Babysitter as Odalisque*

    Sitting before parted
curtains, still as air, she
admires her own even limbs.
When the children have gone
to bed she has nothing but this
waiting. Waiting is window,
ledge, and this wanting to fall, to
rush toward the ground's
pursed lips. In flight, she'd spin
like a starfish, arms and legs
pinwheeling, a wild spiral—
yellow blue and dark.

4. Study for *Searchlight*

    A helicopter encloses
                the neighborhood in its blades'

  rough push / push / push.
      Searchlight slips along windows

  beside the dinner table (crystal
              cuts shadow).

      The hostess is cool as a dime. Hovering
          at the room's edge, she glances

  toward the light gathered in the panes'
                liquid folds.

  She thinks she's seen crossed
lines pressed into her husband's back

        where he lay down in damp grass
with his raspberry-skinned lover.

                  Push /
push. Glare facilitates her escape

through her empty, blinking eye.
    Clatter of roosters preening and crowing,

hens fussing. Push / push / push.
        The helicopter passes, a blue

starfish pinwheeling, moves away.
                         Bloated plates of fruit move

     around the table. Passes again, again away.
            What more could they want?

                 Slender threads of glow stick
in the sills but the fowl are busy and

        do not notice. Push / push. Her skin
smells like burnt coffee and meat

        and something citrusy, maybe limes.
To the room she says

What can they be looking for?

PRAYER FOR THE INSOMNIAC

Let her find it, even
if she's not looking. Let
her sink fast into sleep
on the subway's molded
plastic seat, the city
moving past and through her.
Let it come to her, slouch
into her, a body
sliding into a chair.
Wrap her in the scented
smoke of the cathedral
and intoxicate her with dreams
of martyrs: the sword against
Agnes's throat, Catherine
slipping beneath the wheel,
Pelagia's slow drop
from a slanted rooftop.
Let her lean into sleep
on a late morning park
bench. And let her divine
the annunciation—
Angel, I am afraid—
as she fades there. Let her
forget her reflection
in windows, in pools gathered
on the sunken street when
the eleven o'clock
news asks the city to
forget even itself.
Let her, let her, let her
be swallowed whole by this,
the tremble left to her.

THE SWAY OF ORDINARY LIGHT

    The standard is three minutes,
        a hare's head start, before hounds
            are turned loose from their tangle

        of short leads. This is just one
            sort of beginning (the gun barrel
is another, the scientist's

        slide, another). The pocket
    is full of counterfeit coins
and dice, their edges filed

    and polished—one always rolls
high, the other low. Seven,
        seven. It's easy to switch

dice and palm cards downtown
            in impromptu alley games
        (an ace hidden in a sock, a cross-eyed

            Jack in a hat's band). Three
    minutes: the time it takes
to smooth the pillowcases

    and the corners of the spread
            (a woman, across the street, maybe,
or next door, is seen through her

    window making and remaking
her bed. Sheets lift, sail,
            disappear). The coins feel wrong,

too smooth, like magic beans,
    but they are enough
        for the subway turnstile

and they clink home in the machinery's
metal purse like any other.
             That's another sort

of beginning, the moment
             you know a thing needn't be real:
the scenery waiting

        in the wings for the curtain
to fall, the two-dimensional city, the footlights
that fade to dusk,

          to night. Three minutes: the time it takes
to secure cells under glass and glass
under the microscope's crooked arms.

What lives there is *then*, not *now* or *always*.
        The wail of a hunter's shot
and the change blood makes in air

        are no more than they appear
to be; a lab coat hides nothing
but the doctor's blotchy skin.

The time it takes, the time
        it takes the bus to reach the curb,
hiss open its doors; that is *almost*.

Begin with slip, the sway
        of ordinary light, the trembling
blast furnace, a stairwell, mis-

step and fall and fall and fall.
    The coppery slugs, sometimes,
        jam the machine, leave the hands empty,

    hands intimate with silk and the rattle
of dice. Waking, hands find
    a roll of bills,

a pocket watch, the dark skin
   below the eye.
    The neighbor

   from the backlit window waits now
on a bench for the crosstown bus. Her skirt
  slides above her knee, exposes a bit

    of wild satin against her skin.
 She folds and refolds
her fingers around her fare.

HIGH STREET

reminds her of the bright
atmosphere of panic
the autumn smell of distant

burning; who is and ought to be.
A near-black plum. Some proposal.
Here trumpets sound beneath,

basement cabaret, itch and hunger.
The one who wants genuinely and
so many finds herself vanished

in the narrow light at the city's limit.
She aims to crave nothing
so exotic as blue fruit.

Will the midnight dancers die
of cold? Tangled and smothered
in threads of icy declaration. Quick

the path marked clearly, straight
down the neon brilliant center.
Certain streets hideous as cracks

in the skin. Ignore the pull
of blazing trees in favor
of the sea's green rocking. What

other choice is there? Oh, the sweet
the first bite the flesh broken
and never more perfect.

PECCADILLOES

    A slight fault in
    the paper reveals
    the forgery.
    This is (is this?)
    what they asked for,
    night swimmers, faint
    of breath and ghostly.
    Or the tell
    is in the composition
    of paint. But blue rolls
    into evening in any
    case, little griefs,
    little sins notwith-
    standing. Then again
    the forgettable heat
    of a hand over eyes
    is like that too. Already
    about to dash off to.
    Every truth is there,
    the edge of the brick
    works, the edge
    of town; lies can be
    disguised in driven
    by a pattern of days.
    That vague craving,
    the barest breeze. Keep
    even the smallest betrayal
    distant as a wild past.

SHOULD SALOME APOLOGIZE

Blade slit skin here above my knee and I am sorry it was not an accident (was an accident of timing only, of placement) the silver slipped. Not sorry to have been led (to have followed) behind a curtain of cattail reeds: barely brown rustle and sway no question no *what did you expect* or *what have you done* or *you call this love?* Remorse grows round and fat as a plum.

Horses raise red dust in swelling clouds, endless clouds their running is and moves through. Do you imagine they are sorry for it, for the coming dark, the scarlet-laced shadows of summer dusk, of this particular day? There is no regret in their muscular legs, their manes. Loose from a braid, my hair snags on doornails, low branches. A girl collects these fragments, burns them with my fingernail clippings, my eyelashes, the blood-soaked cotton of my moon-anchored cycle. Fire in a shallow bowl.

I burn like a basket of pinecones, pine needles, sun-bleached boughs. I will wait a lifetime for no apology. I die like this. I am sorry not sorry. I wanted the man's mouth on my skin—lips parted, a kiss, an answer. The setting sun, sore and bruised, is a solution. Horizon (faintly blue crease), the hinge where evening meets tomorrow's edge. I cross my arms over my breasts like a man laid to rest (to sorrow) to rest.

HOLIDAY

Meet the difficult
simplicity of trees

at the end of the street.
Guarantee the second life:

elm-lined suburbia, shameful
season of long-throated

gold-banded silk-sleeved love-
liness. They, the ever present,

how they pretend
not to watch. Slight color,

glossy bits of cloth slipping—
handwristshoulder. Glass to

glass, red red wine, seen
not seen. What is visible

is carnival-sequined and
orange-feathered.

And the crowd swoons.
Already dizzy with lightning.

Consider the nothing
more, the disinherited.

Serene below floorboards,
the faint smell of lake and last

year. The rollaway bed
is a kind speculation. And

what is it, what makes them so sure
we'll ever go anywhere at all?

A BIOGRAPHY OF AMELIA EARHART

1. What Flying Was

Not the blind curve ahead on Ice Mine Road,
taken too fast, firmly held breath, gritty

and hot any cloudless midnight. Not self,
not other (the awful, the brilliant in

between) flick of fin, swift of light bound
to the fish's silver-white belly. Not a summer eclipse.

Not the slip's slender strap, pushed hastily
over the half-moon of her shoulder. Not

the dragonfly that lands on her sunburned forearm—
its body a glassy shiver—but something like

the moment the green insect
put itself down there, like the second

it hovered above her
then came suddenly down; something

like her skin's surprise
at quick, transparent wings.

2. Before the Transatlantic Solo Flight

   Almost everything had already happened.
   She had seen the way mist sometimes
   turns around the end of the runway

   like a vine around a branch until the twist of one
   is indistinguishable from the push of the other.
   This strip is jagged at the margins

   the way she found the window sills
   at the summer cabin—squirrels (soft now
   and rotten) had slipped into the chimney.

   Her hand rested on window frame chewed to splinter.
   She walked haze and uneven edges
   before dawn and thought of the sun lifting itself.

   When the carnival talker called
   "Come in. Come in." Amelia stepped into the cool
   behind the curtain and let her eyes adjust.

   She was not taken; she knew
   what she had seen. Almost everything
   had already happened. Almost everything

   had already happened, so when she saw
   fire on the runway, drew her first breath
   of yellow smoke as it rolled off the wreck—

   steam from a boiling pot, red kitchen curtains
   pushed on spring, the colt's
   uncontrollable lift as he rears, the cresting wave,

   (none of these; all of these)—she knew what she saw.
   She was not fool enough to look away.

3. What Amelia Earhart Saw

    Storefront neon-blue caught curled in some girl's
    hair, her face, chin tilted, composed
    against her own gaze; the pink strand of pearls
    mother's hands turned as she stood, eyes half closed,

    before her mirror; lover's worried tuck
    of lip under lip, suck of cheek and gasp;
    a boy, hairless, wingless, smooth as a bark-
    stripped switch and as uncertain; black flies

    like regrets eye-level, abuzz, circling; mud-
    splashed hooves, legs, belly, and the vanishing
    day; she saw clouds gathered like skirts baring blood-
    less knees, she saw the vast unraveling

    night, she saw reflected in the windscreen
    her own face, gray and metallic as a gun.

ADVICE FOR THE BRIDE

Be keen-eyed.
Be as alluring as ever.
Forget what you wanted

to say. The impossibility
of explaining will settle
on the room like dust.

The rumor it turns
out is true. Or almost.
The key is a care-

ful design, day by day,
the way it all adds up
to a fishbowl full

of ticket stubs and match-
books. Day by day. This,
all the evidence there is.

Flirt into *then what,*
sweetdark and nearly
soundless, *this.*

Flutter of hands. Hips.
Downcast eyes. A bride
can fit her whole breath

inside a crystal vase. Be
so unforgettable. Because
one wants the marvel, the full,

the faultless lips. One wants
a glance backward over
bare shoulder, a yellow jewel

at the throat. See, the dancer's
waist, how it anticipates the hand
that will guide it into the next—

next spin (skirt lifting
to a scalloped edge)
the next perfect turn.

THE ORDINARY HUSBAND

Taboo is nothing to us; we
have traveled some distance. One

house mimics another, room
room doorframe window.

His voice, squat and horizontal.
Pungent. I know what I saw.

Saffron clouds sag into the yard;
it wasn't accidental and it's hardly

a secret. I know what I heard and
the damn voice clings to her hair;

the proposal leaves its peppery
flavor in our nostrils.

Pockets: key and coin, matchbook.
The genuinely miscellaneous contents

of the man. What of it? Sacrament
without fire. On a veranda in a moon-

trance someone's wife drinks
vodka cloudy with lemon juice. Double

tongue. The others, he cracks
like a nutshell between his teeth. He fills

your lungs like you were drowning.
It's difficult for everyone. Certainty,

that's what you get. What will get you.
Comfort of ritual and no surprises. The trip

takes exactly as long as always.
His shadow falls flat. It's October

and it's Thursday. The walk to town,
the red light under the train bridge.

Another mystery of empty hands.
Consider the anger he is subject to.

The night is lonely as a hotel
and clear; the blue pill

smells like its plastic bottle. It is
likely he has forgotten, again.

UPON CROSSING THE THRESHOLD, THE BRIDE

The rhythm here, in thirds, in waltz-
time, like a mumbled *one two
three one two three,* pulses there

a subtle thrum in back of it all.
Wait at the window (curtains
just parted, still more light, yes,

there must be). Apartment: eight rooms,
a suspension bridge above soaked
bus stop corner. A woman stands

in a doorway, framed
and familiar. Hers is the city
of heavy rain and watchful border.

White wall, open cabinet door.
Consider the narrative:
parable of the neighborhood

charade, derelict porches and ruined
language. And the broken-toothed dog,
so easily misunderstood, so quickly

spent. Consider the curse of threes.
The floor slopes toward the mantel along
the room's interior edge. There again

the girl two stories below,
her pleated skirt swirling
on the artificial breeze of a passing truck,

the indistinct reflection
of cars on wet pavement.
The building will not collapse

into quiet. At the end of this street
pattern shifts up the pitch of gray hill—blue air,
shadow—and still this blinking

façade wears its game face, holds
itself solid. Amplified traffic.
She: unmoved, asks for nothing.

Headlights trace an arch across
the plain, the determined fourth wall.
Stands in a doorway without asking.

PYRAMID

    Can't you see it, the blue-
    edged girls all twist and tumble? How lush
    the grass that lovingly accepts their figures.

    Doesn't it please you, their aesthetic collapse,
    how, for a moment, they flutter like dandelion seeds?
    The top-most girl falls

    often—from curbs, over tree
    roots, almost anything might send her.
    From any altitude the fall is pitch and roll

    and to the one in flight, it's
    a reminder that a body must reach
    for whatever might hold—a wrist,

    the front yard oak, any doorjamb.
    She's grown accustomed to the movement
    of air around her mutable frame; nothing is enough

    to stay her, to prevent the faller's seasick sway
    at the top of the staircase. The body, still
    clutching the wrought iron banister, starts

    to lurch, to spill
    limbs into *crack* and *ah*. This is
    the miniature of the crowd's cry

    when the red-sequined girl
    slides through the hands of the man
    hanging by his knees.

    The thud against one's own
    wooden stairs of hip, shoulder,
    temple is a foreign voice: *I—I—*

I am. I am. Falling. Like the downward
stroke of a paintbrush, like a river turned
cataract. People who fall

find each other by bends where
bones didn't heal right, by scabs,
by swellings and scars and

white, white bandages
that spread over joints
or, when loosened, wag

like signal flags one might
wave overhead as welcome
or warning. The cheerleader

joins crowds gathered about
daily tragedies. Today they watch
an apartment fire; a man throws

a framed photo, a pocket watch
from a third story window. He must
follow. The girl thinks she'll know

if he fell or if he jumped. Gravity has
taught her something: the difference
between action and reaction. The man

waits, arms extended like a balancing pole.
The one foot forward, poised,
anticipates the wire's small give.

SHE ASKS

The dead, immense. Her search is spoon-like, dipped
in swirl and ripple, or second thoughts. Girl, yet bare-
ly: ear or mouth—a gooseberry moon kept
under a palm, each pocket wide as where

and here and *Oh*. Or hark back to between
fist and coin. The brooder's light well under
(not red, not gold—what lends the space its green?)
the girl's one soupy eye. Do you wonder

what sort of that she is? That's enough. Catch
her breath and you will. Back to her thumb-head
birds: they're almost. But that's a perfect latch
on her up-most door. Blindly. No. Instead

we watch serene and yellow fruits, their swell
to humanness. She asks and they just swell.

HOUSE GEOMETRY

    Count steps from the door, calculate
        distance to the narrow
kitchen, to the bed. Study of surfaces,
        shapes: discipline of two bodies
in the glare from arched
        window. Who will die first?
Shoes behind the chimney, St. Ruth
        blessing doorways, the broken mirror
turned to the wall. To grasp
        the properties of space because
and let's not forget certain
        elements remain invariant. Always
other things happen. And the crack
        crosses the whole of the white ceiling,
the length of the bedroom wall. She will not
        survive him. Bend toward measurement,
seduction of points, angles right or acute.
        Promise shines everywhere
in the still the glassy oasis capital
        where rows of houses like this
(usual model, usual box and triangle
        of a child's drawing) sit even and
steady, are without suggestion. Has it always
        been like this? A secret can be kept
inside the square pocket
        in the lining of a husband's coat.
This is no kind of science.

SALOME'S ANSWER

May your eyes recede, with the waning
moon, to rest behind their sockets. May
dawn's design, that braid of red light above this
city, be lost on you. And may your ears go deaf;
and may your tongue sag mute behind broken
teeth. Feel your fingers snapped in two by September
wind. Wait in the unbroken cavity of your skull
for a dream of the one heart you love. Sense its
    pulse, its thump
thump, thump from behind the walls of the scientist's
jar. In its own chemical dream, the heart
pounds almost strong enough
to crack the glass. Hour by hour, may it grow
slow, grow quiet, until it is as still as
the hell between your ribs.

APOLOGY FOR NEW WIVES

The hoax of relic bones
and the goddess of hinges
stay buried in the still
frozen ground. A scheme
luminous as a pearl.
Hidden: flimsy telegrams
and torn-envelope letters,
clear-eyed jewels; all of it
bundled, pushed deep
into a hole in the wall,
nestled among sparrows.
This is a hard fact:
appetites make bad wives.
Cigarette smoke swirls white,
rooms forget dimensions.
The birds begin to escape.
They leave almost no trace
in the electric morning;
they shine like silver keys.

SALOME AND JOHN THE BAPTIST

    Salome sliced afternoon
    fruit; one then
    another   she split

    skin of yellow sweet
    lemons   with her thumb-
    nail   (the body:

    lightning-cracked
    trunk). Sword axe   silver
    knife   blade there again

    and again there
    where the blood   now
    is dry   there the body

    became a clay jar.
    If a crowd gathered to watch
    cleaver hatchet   the man

    work, Salome didn't   notice. She
    cut the meat
    of a white melon   sun

    sliding   westward
        horizonward and
    she reminded herself

    that the richest man said
    I've been thinking
    of you. The skin of her

    fingers softened,
    puckered   (a mouth)
    from handling sour-sweet

pulp and flesh.
   Salome was   surprised
how easily she

said   *no,* how she walked
away without
looking back   he called

her   her name
a warning   a man
shouting to a boy gone

too far on thin ice (John's arms
grow rigid, free of their
days and   the stain now

his blood   now
larger than his
body,   blood moving like

ripples rolling   out
from   the moment a
stone meets   water's

surface) pink figs   green
figs   yellow grapes from
prickly   vines. Clear

juice purple   figs.
It was easy
to give   away her

secret   *you have   nothing to give me.*
Nothing   *I want.*
Salome   never looked

at the axe or   its achievement
there   where rain   sometimes
fell   left lopsided

black circles
on swept earth.
Alone all   afternoon, Salome

knew the sound of her
voice sometimes
    emptied the house.

OFF AT THE HINGES

If you're like her you
wake some days to a mirage

of suburban lawn, kaleidoscopic
sprinklers, turn and tick. Blue

in this light, trees go
sky wild, are good enough.

Will have to do. Remember
the day's edge, the corner pine

drained of sap, the handfuls
of grass. Yesterday over and

done. Voice, bluster and
hitch, can't find its objective.

Come on in before the
streetlights turns to remedy.

When she finds the door
off at the hinges she won't

do a thing about it. The gap,
better than that clutch of blades.

What she leans into. Not
the unspecified apprehension,

its mossy taste. No. Only
the shadow that locates her.

KEYS

lowest note; list of solutions (as in: "the Master used a");
the hold which plaster has on a wall;
a pin, bolt or wedge (as in: a cotter); a cardinal
point; vibrating steel tongues; spiritual authority
(as in: "the Bishop's" or "the Spiritual Power
of the"); primary claw of a hawk's foot.

common in phrases and proverbs (such as: "to the
street," "as cold as a," "and book").

•

Marigold custard: crush 1 cup of marigold petals; mix with salt, sugar, nutmeg. Scald 3 cups of milk with 2 vanilla beans and an egg yolk. Combine with dry ingredients. Cool before serving.

•

Wives' Tales: Too many
carrots will turn your
skin orange (true: palms
and the soles of feet).
Vinegar will dry
up all your blood (not true).

•

I served divorce papers to suited and severe men and women every Friday in July. I once chased a woman three blocks, waving her bulky envelope. Her red blazer flapped behind her like a cape. By block two I was gaining. She wasn't one of those pumps-in-handbag-gym-shoes-to-work types. She had no idea how to run. That was during the city's dry spell and hydrants

were opened all over; they bubbled like picture-book
fountains. Imagine that.

•

black-canal. blue-ferry
route. yellow-rail-
road. green-bridge. red-snow
emergency. double
green-covered bridge.

•

From a distance, a dead sheep and a dead deer
look about the same. If a sheep dies
when the ground is frozen, you can
haul it out to the highway, dump it,
drive off, and almost no one will notice.

•

I shine shoes on the busiest corner
in Philadelphia. I draw a circle on each

cheek with discarded apricot lipstick. My mother
has moved to a leaf-shaped island where storms lift

dogs and even cars right off the ground, plant
them, sometimes, miles away.

There's a gray leaf pressed
to the windshield. It's stuck

in the wiper blade whining
across glass. Back, forth, back.

Now they're calling for rain.

CURSING THE EQUATOR

a story she'd tell lying down
handprint on glass or in drying
mud red impression where fingers
closed on her upper arm the inexact
shape of that memory

•

numbered crosslines on the map lines
announcing here and now but
she does not consent there are so many
false maps so many liars

•

she curses the fish their
eyes blood-pink their singing
she has forgotten
whether the sea lies
beyond the door of this
rented room or another she
curses hot hours her lover
gone crazy with fever she
watches him breathe
and curses his mouth

•

invisible bite of a silvery
equatorial beetle or exotic
germ whatever draws streaks
across his face pulls cracks on
his moving still moving
lips slips under her skin
too only cool this time

•

ignore lines across
palm ignore the girl in a bar
saying *lifeline loveline* touching
every outstretched hand
with the same gesture

•

dogs lick her ankles her dress pink
as her earlobe slides higher
on her thigh and not by chance no
that wasn't this cliff city
there were no beetles no conjure girl
kids collected bottle caps
and dogs wandered loose in alleys
and seagulls somewhere
somewhere nearby but not here

•

the maps are wrong the streets
named twice or not at all the outlines
of water askew

•

dream a transatlantic plane
above this imagined seam but first
Amelia Earhart stands on the runway
beside the shining body shining
wings of the exotic equatorial beetle
she waves like a beauty queen lips closed
against the gap in her front teeth

•

she curses black-leafed trees
the sleepwalker the deaf boy signing
at the counter in the grocery curses
the line across the middle of everything

•

near circle of nipple near
circle of navel walk the edge
the straightest street in town
her lips sun swollen blister
back burns red until
sunlight on her shoulders
bends her into an arch

•

air moves in
response only to
her hand fanning his
face her face and
to the open close open
of the room's blue door

THE CATHERINE WHEEL

Hers was the power of embers after fire: power of reduction, the persuasion of a thing left behind, forgotten. **Presumably, Catherine of Alexandria lived during the fourth century. There is no ancient cult of this saint, no mention in early martyrologies, no early works of art. Her tortures consisted of being broken on a wheel, but the machine broke down, injuring bystanders.** There was a world before the wheel, before the hub and spokes, before the rim and sharpened spikes. But all who saw it knew the wheel was a world unto itself. It was a bulging sun, a plucked eye; the wheel was the shape of Catherine's mouth as she began to pray: *O my God, forgive*.... Before the wheel there were the even folds of the red gown, the slim gold ring, the crown and fist.

The details of her mythical legend make her a noble girl who Bride of Christ, how easily you told the Emperor No, said *love* **despised marriage to the Emperor,** *is not found in your crooked limbs,* **who was persecuted for her Christianity,** *your salty flesh.* He watched you fold your hands, watched your mouth move in whispered devotion, watched sunlight catch in your yellow hair. **who disputed successfully with fifty philosophers** He wanted, at once, both to lie encircled by your watery hair and to break **called in to convince her of the errors of Christianity.** your forehead against a round and perfect stone.

Her intercession was valued because she was considered to be (a) the bride of Christ, (b) the successful advocate who triumphed over the philosophers, (c) the protectress of the dying. Catherine, after your death, pools of water collected everywhere you had ever knelt in prayer. Women who press their palms to these pools are blessed with visions of you holding a fragment of the broken wheel, your hair spinning on wind. Crows and ravens drink at these pools and become monarch butterflies. (O, power of reduction.) **Sixty-two churches were dedicated to her and 170 medieval bells still bear her name.** The air above is filled with gold.

The wheel is **The cult began** a paper globe, and it is **in the 9th century at Mount Sinai, to which her body** a hoop a child pushes with a stick. **was supposed to have been transported by 'angels' though** The wheel is the bear trap's gaping mouth, **this may have been a misinterpretation of 'monks,' often described in antiquity as living an 'angelic' life.** it is a loop of rope, a ship's porthole, the footprints left from circles danced on a dirt floor.

When the wheel failed, the Emperor ordered Catherine beheaded. Milk instead of blood flowed from her severed head. The Catherine Wheel is the gears of a clock, turning. Your body should have been crushed bone by bone: shattered ankles, shins, kneecaps. **She is the patron of young girls, of students (especially philosophers and apologists), of nurses (because milk instead of blood flowed from her severed head),** He would have settled for a fraction of your worship; **of spinners and millers and wheelwrights.** your broken bones would become the wanting V's of birds' mouths. When the wheel cracked, splintered, split into a hundred pieces, your eyes searched the crowd for the Emperor, held him steadily in your gaze as he spoke.

FRESH PAINT IN EVERY ROOM

A makeshift attic room three stories
above grass baked yellow; this
is no easy coast. The air

brittle, her breath a snapping
branch. The paint, a shade recalling
the end beginning again, trees

gone bare and bare. Her skin is
damp with the memory of her
fifteen-year-old self. These hands

unrecognizable. That wanting.
All wrong: almost the same color
as the shadow inside her mouth.

Sometimes one finds an abandoned house.
July and everything heat cracked. Seams
in wooden floors, thin skin of her lips, vague

shape seen from the corner of her eye.
The windows painted shut and vaguely
rippling. The street waits while the sun

centers itself. Is anything more beautiful
than the truck carrying sheets of glass, traveling
suddenly, slowly past a house on an empty street,

a woman in a half painted room?
The fragile arrangement all blue
at the seams; barely discernible

reflections, gone before she can
make them out. Dizzy, the thralldom
of paint fumes, she thinks

about fingers. And tongues, and
the smooth backs of a girl's thighs.
This is a certain kind of elsewhere.

She grows hot and lightheaded; brushstrokes
and breath and almost but never quiet.
She is confused about who remembers this.

WINDOWS

Half-heard words are barefoot boys, picking their way through the alley to the corner of King and Highland. They are careless, stumbling, gone into the dark. Windows, if you let them, slink off to where the stone drive meets the road. They wear whatever light they can grab hold of. A habit of squinting against the glare, separating shape from shadow, has resulted in this argument, this shrewd-hearted room. The clock's silver hands are folded in exasperation or appeal and the neighborhood is dreadful without voices. I burnt my tongue sipping coffee on a brick porch and the screen door slapped shut behind you. Our house is only edges and angles; it is the crook of an arm, the joint where bone meets bone. The door swings open at even the slightest knock. Windows frame the street from here, the room from there; the panes throw pale streaks toward every corner. My hands fit over the day like a glass over a cricket. Bristly legs bow into trill and trill, not song but broken bits of it. Look, this ugly, this fine form is nothing I've ever seen before.

SALOME MEANS *PEACE BE WITH YOU*

I was called *Golden Eye Red*
Mouth Precious and I am not afraid
of a man with a crooked spine. And I am not
afraid of that fiery tree cradling
each word in the hollow joint of trunk and
limb: the burning ironwood—insipid
flowers and glossy leaves, all
of it up in smoke. I was called *Bird*
Singer Moon Gone Child. I was called
The One Who Burns the Black Ironwood.
In still tongue hours or in hours of silvery
fishtailed lies I pace the same floor, breathe
this green sandalwood air (perfume
an eighth veil). The tree will burn
and burn, will go slowly, will vanish
to cinder glow. Smoke tree, cloud tree, tree
of forgetfulness, I am not afraid of tongue
hours licking by, of being kissed
in this house where blossoms sick
with fragrance bend almost in half.
When I lay down the crackling
ironwood calls me, calls *Swift River Sweet*
Voice Hush-Hush, a feverish solution, my old name.

OPEN HOUSE

>The neighborhood approaches
>a watery balance, simple
>ebb and flow; its women
>
>cultivate a cold enthusiasm
>for the overheard.
>A cipher in the slanting
>
>afternoon sun, reason revolves
>like an instrument.
>Moss climbs the walls,
>
>greens the perfect
>day-filled kitchen.
>Familiar path of
>
>clock hands: a close room
>and roses and too much
>conversation. Relentless
>
>charm leaves the housewives
>translucent; they turn lovely
>backs toward the door.
>
>Ears burn, heels of hands wear
>red half moons where fingernails
>wouldn't quit. November's

violence will erase lines
from skin until each becomes
smooth as an egg. And their

seeking mouths gape,
empty sweet and aching.
The wives twist in their tea cups,

screw slender black heels into plush
carpet. A camera lens turns open
wide and wide to eat more light.

EVERYWHERE AT ONCE

1.
Syllables tell me a trouble.

And when the gray fog rolls
up from the freezing the not quite
frozen river, no one here
can remember why they came.

Some debts cannot be repaid.

2.
Parched laughter from the TV in the next apartment
stiff-backed kitchen chair
and the mirror on the back of the door
and the wreath of hair in the drain
and the green apples
and steadily burning coffee
and black ink scrawled on the back of the newspaper
and the hollow, relentless desire to steal something:
this, the room on the ridge above the tracks. This
and the train's brassy all-night whistle.

3.
black thread keeps the birds out

but Goddamn
if she doesn't start
telling the same story
again, the tenth time today,
again and this time she even

4.
Winter threatens
to sing. In this city
the people sleep surrounded

by reddish not-
light; eyes not
closed. Not quite.

Will the great white phone never ring?

5.
she is / looking / she / is
for / looking / a fine woolen
coat / it might / because
it might start / snowing / to
snow / any time now / and
she's / she is / looking
for a lucky charm /
lucky / for a reasonable
dress / a red / a red
lipstick / looking
for keys to / a key to
the door / this door /
for keys / for a charm

6.
And the crows on the railing
and the smoke alarm disconnected months ago
and the jacket on its hook
and shouting from the apartment next door
after midnight, even after all that rain.

7.
The water pitcher at the table's center
is little more than bowl and handle.
Knock it over and it is everywhere

at once, every wanting turned liquid,
a picture window.

8.
says *I probably already
told you* but that doesn't
stop her and it wasn't
even interesting
the first time, and anyway
she says *and So
I'm looking still, looking for*

9.
Dream of dream
of sleek fish
bones and wake
to no one
at the sink washing
with yellow soap no
one in the doorway
or on the front step.

THE WIFE OF THE LEFT HAND

    is on the bed
    sweating; without
    and still. Hurricane
    of afternoon, lingering
    smell of seaweed
    it must be August. She,
    there, the bed beneath
    her. Everything slight-
    ly hazy. The body, no
    good house, wants what it
    wants; does not listen.
    Careless breath, all wave
    and sky, sneaks
    under her eyelid. She
    pretends not to hear
    the persistent knock
    on the screen door.

GHOST TOWN

    I am the square of light that falls
        on the pears in the basket.

    I am the white sphere of the plate.

    I am the honeysuckle held to your flat tongue, the
        sugary drop.

    I am the far away sound
        of cars crossing a joint in the blacktop.

    I am the subtle nick of a needle and I am
        the bottle's stout neck.

    I am the splinter beneath your skin (hushed
        voice repeating *throb* and *ache*).

    I am the miniature peacock feather pinned to
        the silk band of the bride's blue hat.

    I am the leaves twisted to braid the flowers, and I am
        the unexpected weight of the boughs.

    I am the waves past the high dunes, crash and
        pull, the salt air; and I am the water's
        surface, gray-green and still out of sight.

    I am the crack and snap of wind in a ship's halyards or
        a flag at half mast.

    I am the doctor's cold hands, pressed to
        your belly, your ribs, your spine.

    I am the body you reach for at midnight, the body
        you reach for in the gray hour before day.

    Who were you the night the pavement split and slid?

The night fire cracked the earth open and I
   fell into its mouth?

Who were you when uneven air shook the wings?

Who were you when first frost broke the branches?

And who are you now, as the last of the birds
   cranes his neck to look?

And now, turning a flawless plum in your hands;
   and after (lips and teeth and tongue)
   the sweet red bite?

Who will you be when the rooms are empty?

When wind swings the door wide?

ACKNOWLEDGEMENTS

The bold text in "The Catherine Wheel" is adapted from the *Oxford Dictionary of Saints*.

Grateful acknowledgment is made to the editors of the following publications in which versions of some of these poems have appeared: *AGNI, canwehaveourballback, The Card Catalog Poetry Project, Colorado Review, The Connecticut Review, Cream City Review, Drunken Boat, Fence, Free Verse, The Journal, Kiosk, The Laurel Review, The Little Critic, Mandorla, Mankato Poetry Review, Painted Bride Quarterly, Phoebe, The Poker, Quarter After Eight, Salt Hill Journal, Shearsman, Sow's Ear Poetry Review,* and *Verse.*

AUTHOR

Nancy Kuhl's chapbook, *In the Arbor,* was winner of the Wick Poetry Chapbook Prize and was published by Kent State University Press. She is co-editor of Phylum Press, an independent publisher of innovative poetry (www.phylumpress.com).

www.ingramcontent.com/pod-product-compliance
Lightning Source LLC
Chambersburg PA
CBHW030048100426
42734CB00037B/654